Hi Jokes ... I'm Dad

The definitive collection of paternal humor (Dad Jokes)

VOLUME 1

Craig Stilley

Copyright © 2022 Craig Stilley

All rights reserved.

ISBN:9798413071625

DEDICATION

To my family, who have suffered through my humor over the years and without whom I would not have a reason to put this together, or for that matter do anything else. My son Tyler and my daughter Alexa, without them I would not be a dad. And, of course, my wife and partner in all things Stephanie. While I may have the Dad Jokes, she is the wonderful mother for our children.

CONTENTS

	Acknowledgments	i
1	General Humor…	Pg 1
2	Offering Sympathy…	Pg 11
3	Conquering Your Fears…	Pg 15
4	There's Nothing Like Family…	Pg 17
5	Better Check on Grandpa…	Pg 21
6	AHHH Love…	Pg 23
7	Our Furry Friends… and Their Friends…	Pg 27
8	The Doctor is in…	Pg 31
9	It's a Living…	Pg 35
10	To Serve and Protect…	Pg 37
11	I Should Have Paid Attention in School…	Pg 41
12	ARRRGGHH Matey…	Pg 45
13	A Matter of Trust…	Pg 49
14	…Walked into a Bar…	Pg 51
15	Truly Bad…	Pg 55
16	It's a Thinker…	Pg 59

ACKNOWLEDGMENTS

To all who listened to my humor and provided copious amounts of eye rolling so that I knew what was funny, and what wasn't. (though some may still say I cannot tell the difference). My immediate family Stephanie, Tyler, and Alexa (the best free book editor out there); my extended family: my mother Bonny; my stepmother Kit; my brother Bill; Lexi and Sri; and all my current and past co-workers. Thank you for enduring my comments and attempts at humor over the years.

Cover by Sri Kandula. Editing and Formatting by Alexa Stilley

GENERAL

HUMOR...

I rarely tell dad jokes...

                      but when I do, he laughs.

What do Winnie the Pooh and Alexander the Great have in common...

                      Same middle name.

I was walking into a store and a clown held the door for me...

                      What a nice jester!

What is the difference between a poorly dressed man on a bicycle, and a well-dressed man on a unicycle...

                      attire.

Why do scuba divers jump backwards into the water?...

    If they jumped forward, they would still be in the boat.

Sometimes I tuck my knees into my chest and lean forward...

    that's just how I roll.

I bought a vacuum cleaner six months ago and I'm not sure I like it...

    Since it has only been collecting dust.

Why shouldn't you write with a dull pencil...

                              it's pointless.

I went to a baseball game, and I wondered why the ball looked like it was getting bigger and bigger...

                              and then it hit me.

I had a garage sale and got rid of all my dead batteries...

                                free of charge.

I hate it when I am the only one without hand sanitizer...

> my friends are always rubbing it in.

My friend accused me of being a plagiarist...

> His words, not mine.

Thank you, student loans, for getting me through college...

> I don't think I can ever repay you.

My friend says he likes quilts more than duvets...

> I told him to not be so quick to make blanket statements like that.

I started reading a suspenseful book in Braille. Something bad is going to happen....

> I can feel it.

A lot of problems in the old western towns could have been avoided...

> if cowboy planners had just made towns big enough for everyone.

Did you hear about the corduroy pillow?...

        It's making headlines everywhere.

Where do you go if you are hurt in a peekaboo accident?...

        The I.C.U.!

I bought a pen that can write underwater...

        and many other words.

Unfortunately, I used to be addicted to soap...

        but I am clean now.

Soviet Union Joke: A Soviet citizen was told that the plumber would not be able to visit him until 10 years from now on April 2nd. The citizen asked, "Morning or evening?" He is asked why that matters? The citizen replies…

"Well, the electrician is coming in the morning."

Quite a set up:

A man is driving a train around a bend near a town when it suddenly de-rails and kills several people. They hold a trial and the man is found guilty of negligence and receives the death penalty. They put him in an electric chair and throw the switch... Nothing happens. The authorities are perplexed and reach out for help from scientists at the local university. They investigate and come to find out...

                   He was just a poor conductor.

OFFERING

SYMPATHY...

I saw a woman who was sad, so I asked her if I could offer a few good words. She said, "Sure."...

I said, "Bargain." She said...

"Thanks, that means a great deal to me."

I said, "Infinity." She said...

"Thanks, that means more than you could possibly imagine."

I said, "Earth." She said...

"Thanks, that means the world to me."

I said, "Gorgeous." She said...

        "Thanks, that's beautiful."

I said, "Sugar." She said...

        "Thanks, that is so sweet."

I said, "Sufficient." She said...

        "Thanks, I think that's enough."

CONQUERING

YOUR FEARS...

I used to have a fear of escalators...

        but I am taking steps to avoid it.

I used to have a fear of speed bumps...

        but I am slowly getting over it.

I was afraid my quilt was keeping a secret from me...

        turns out it was just a cover up.

I was going to buy a book on phobias...

        but I was afraid it wouldn't help.

THERE'S NOTHING

LIKE FAMILY…

My sister met her boyfriend who worked at the zoo, and when she saw him in his uniform...

        she knew he was a keeper.

My brother and I now laugh at how competitive we were growing up...

        But I laugh more.

My son told me he did not understand cloning. I explained...

        "That makes two of us."

My son asked me, "Why is that book so thick?"...

        I replied, "It's a long story."

During some tough financial times I put my boy on my lap and said, "Son...

        someday we will have 2 chairs."

BETTER CHECK

ON GRANDPA...

I will never forget what my grandfather said before he kicked the bucket...

"Watch how far I can kick this bucket!"

My grandfather started walking 5 miles a day when he turned 70...

Now we don't know where he is.

My father's final words, "Pints, Liters, Gallons."...

that spoke volumes to me.

AHHH

LOVE...

You should never date a tennis player...

                       love means nothing to them.

I once fell in love with a girl who only knew four vowels...

    Unfortunately, she did not even know 'I' existed.

I said, "bless you," when my ex-wife sneezed...

    Now she is Looking around the bushes wondering who said that.

My wife was screaming during labor so I asked, "What's wrong?" She said the contractions were killing her. So I said...

"What IS wrong?"

My wife and I went to a therapist and he told us to embrace our mistakes...

so she gave me a hug.

If at first you don't succeed...

then do it how your wife told you.

My wife tripped while carrying a basket of ironed clothes. There was nothing I could do...

                        but watch it all unfold.

My wife is tired of my dad jokes. I asked her what I should do to stop. She said, "Whatever means necessary." I replied...

                        "No, it doesn't."

OUR FURRY FRIENDS...

AND THEIR FRIENDS...

Ever notice that when geese fly in a V that one side is longer than the other...

> That is because there are more geese on that side.

What does a fish say when he runs into a wall?...

> "Dam!"

How do you tell if an ant is male or female? Put them in a cup of water, and if they sink, they are a girl ant and...

> if they float, they are boy ant (buoyant).

Two fish are in a tank. One looks at the other and says...

"Do you know how to drive this thing?"

THE DOCTOR

IS IN...

I hurried to the doctor because I thought I was shrinking. The doctor says, "Slow down and we will make an appointment...

    For now, you'll have to be a little patient."

When someone passes away, what part of their body part goes last?...

    the pupils, they dilate.

Guess who I bumped into on the way to get my glasses...

    everybody. *(I bet you didn't see that coming)*

"I've got some good news and some bad news," said my doctor. Sadly, I replied, "Give me the good news."...

"They are going to name a disease after you."

A doctor walks into the examining room with a solemn look on his face. He says, "You're dying, and you don't have much time left." The patient says, "How long do I have?" The doctor says, "10." The patient is confused and says, "10 months, 10 years?"...

The doctor replies, ... "9..."

It's a Living...

My brother got fired from a calendar factory...

        he took a week off.

At first, I refused to believe that my father, a highway worker, was a thief. But when I got home...

        all the signs were there.

Why are pilots nervous...

        their jobs are always up in the air.

Mirror inspector...

        I could see myself in that job.

To Serve

And Protect...

Someone is stealing the wheels off police cars...

> The cops are working tirelessly to catch them.

And unfortunately...

> the cars were forced into early retirement.

When I was younger, I fought off an armed robber at my store with a pricing gun. The police put out an alert...

> for a 6-foot-tall man with a price on his head.

A hole was dug outside our town station...

        the police are looking into it.

Someone stole all the toilets from our local station. Unfortunately...

        the police have nothing to go on.

Someone robbed equipment from the K9 kennel...

        the police say they haven't got any leads.

The police caught two people who stole a calendar...

                                    they each got 6 months.

I SHOULD HAVE PAID ATTENTION IN SCHOOL…

My teacher asked me, "What is the meaning of ignorance and apathy?" I replied...

        "I don't know and I don't care."

In school my teacher always told me that 'icy' is an easy word to spell. Looking back now...

        i see why.

A Mexican magician told his audience he would disappear on the count of three. He counted. "Uno... Dos..."

        and then disappeared without a Tres.

When I was young, I asked my teacher, "Are 'well' and 'actually' single syllable words?" She replied...

                    "Well yes, but actually no."

ARRRGGHH

MATEY...

Where do pirates get their hooks?...

                     the second-hand store.

What's a pirate's favorite fast-food restaurant?...   Arrrrby's?...

                    nope, it's Long John Silvers.

What letter keeps a pirate happy?...

              It's P. Without that he is irate.

What's a pirate's favorite letter?... R?...

    You'd think so, but his first love is the sea (C).

What is a pirate's least favorite letter?...

'Dear sir or madam, Your IP address has been flagged for illegally downloading movies..."

A MATTER

OF TRUST...

I don't trust atoms...

        They make up everything

I don't trust people who use graph paper...

        They're always plotting something.

I don't trust stairs...

        they're always up to something.

...WALKED INTO A BAR...

Three conspiracy theorists walk into a bar...

> You can't tell me that's just coincidence.

Two men walked into a bar...

> the woman ducked.

A man walked into the bar, and says, "Teepee wigwam, teepee wigwam, teepee wigwam." The bartender says...

> "Relax, your two tents."

A man is staying upstairs at an old-fashioned Inn and comes downstairs to the pub. The bartender challenges him to a trivia contest with his chicken. If he wins, he gets a wish. He accepts but says that Spanish is his first language. The Bartender says that the chicken speaks Spanish also. The chicken wins easily, answering in Spanish. The man is sad he did not get his wish but is still impressed with the smart animal. He tells the bartender he did not anticipate such an eventful night. The bartender says...

"No one expects the Spanish Inn quiz wish hen."

TRULY BAD...

OTHERWISE KNOWN AS "I'M SORRY"

How many people does it take to change a lightbulb?...

> Is just one of the questions I should have asked before buying a lighthouse.

3 men on a boat with 4 cigarettes, but they don't have a way to light them. How do they smoke?...

> Toss one cigarette overboard to make the boat a cigarette lighter.

Why did the kraken destroy all 4 ships carrying spuds?...

> no one can eat just one potato ship.

If only: Yoda's last name was...

                                                        layheehooo.

In the 1600's, a cold air balloon is invented. A novel idea...

                                      but it never took off.

My friend wanted a hair piece and was told it would cost $100. Sounds like a lot but it is really...

                                A very small price toupee.

How do you spell panda...

                                           just need p and a.

I once spent $300 on a limo ride, but that did not include a driver! So...

All that money spent and nothing to chauffeur it.

Many puns make me feel numb. But math puns...

make me feel number.

How do you keep your dog from barking in the back seat?...

put him in the front seat.

It's A

Thinker...

Online shopping can be frustrating. I tried to search 'lighters,'...

    and all I got was 12,634 matches.

I was going to tell a joke about time travel...

    but you guys didn't like it.

What do you call a stolen Tesla...

    an Edison.

There are three types of people in the world...

those who are good at math and those who aren't.

What is it called when you have second thoughts about a pre-planned trip to Native American land?...

          A reservation reservationreservation.

If there is a bi-partisan agreement in Congress that marijuana should be allowed to be used for body pain...

    Then there is joint support for joint support for joint support.

My friend gave me an elephant figurine as a housewarming gift for my living room. I thanked him, and he said...

          "Don't mention it."

When is a joke a 'Dad' joke...

                  when it becomes apparent.

ABOUT THE AUTHOR

Craig is a certified 'dad' with two wonderful children whohave always been good enough to acknowledge him to their friends despite the continuous stream of 'humor'. He is also an MBA with a resume of successful management positions at a variety of companies. Craig is a military vet who has lived in multiple places, both within the U.S. and abroad. Craig's background has led to a unique speaking style which include Spanglish and both northern and southern vernacular. He has even been heard to utter the phrase, "It's wicked y'all."

Made in the USA
Coppell, TX
07 August 2022